Silent Beauty *Speaks*

A Quiet Collection of Poems

Margaret Wade

ISBN 979-8-89043-502-6 (paperback)
ISBN 979-8-89043-503-3 (digital)

Copyright © 2024 by Margaret Wade

All rights reserved. No part of this publication may be reproduced, distributed, or transmitted in any form or by any means, including photocopying, recording, or other electronic or mechanical methods without the prior written permission of the publisher. For permission requests, solicit the publisher via the address below.

Christian Faith Publishing
832 Park Avenue
Meadville, PA 16335
www.christianfaithpublishing.com

Printed in the United States of America

Acknowledgments

I want to thank my friends and family for their faithful support and encouragement in my writing of these beautiful poems, which I hope will uplift and inspire. I want to especially thank Ken, Susie, and Matt for encouraging me to publish my work. Without them and the loving support of others, I would not have been emboldened to share my work with a public audience.

Introduction

As I think about the way inspiration sometimes hits like a tidal wave or whispers like a gentle breeze, I think of what inspires me to write poetry. It is the beauty that surrounds me, both within and without. It is the essence of living, the truth of both physical and spiritual reality. It is the wonder that emanates from every corner of nature and every step of reality. It is the awe I feel for God's creation and the unshakable praise that leaps to my pen as I write words that fall short of describing the glories, both great and small, that surround me day to day. I hope this book of poems reflects just a small part of what I feel when I see the living world.

Sunrise Poems

A Marbled Sky

When first I rose, and laid my eyes
Upon the marbled sunrise,
The moving clouds of dark and gold,
I saw a story yet untold
The expectation of the day
A light to hold, to hope, and pray
May I find grace enough today

Setting Gold

The setting gold,
That liquid pool of light
So bottomless and pure
Too bright for eyes, the brilliant orb
Of life sinks down beneath its fold
Gathering its strands of light
Till only dusk and dark remain.

The empty sky mourns deeply the loss
Of that which clothed its nakedness
With vivid colors of delight
That lit the world with life and light
That caused the creatures' heads to rise
And wonder at the great horizon.

With mournful sighs, the darkness waits
Eagerly seeking heaven's gates
To open wide with bursting song
The morning anthem sung aloud
Accompanied by glory proud.

How long?
Cries darkness with despair
How long till every hurt and care
Is stunned by heaven's golden joy
And all is lost in light's array?

The dark awaits the rush of day
When faith springs free, and fear away
The cold and emptiness subside
And hope and living life abide.

The Last Blush

Twilight:
As the sinking sun dips below the horizon,
The last blush,
The rosy flame,
Flares into the cloudless blue,
Desperate to portray one last glimpse
Of glory before departing below.

It rises,
Filling the air,
Tinting the trees with color,
Overwhelming the sky with spectacle.

It grows,
Spreading till it forms a rosy ring
Around the horizon.

It stays,
Holding its breath,
Clinging to the last shred of hope.

Then it deepens,
Fades,
And dies away.
Twilight ends in dusk and darkness.

Up Comes Gold

Up comes gold
That rising tide
Of sunlight
Heralding brilliant day!

The rising blush
Blooms full and bright
Banishing fear
And nature's night

The rising day
Arrayed in light
Reveals the beauty
Of that sight
We see upon each morning's dawn
The riches of the earth
Blessings in spite
Of all the pain and sorrow, baring
Graces from our tender, caring
Sovereign Maker of all things
Whose wonders all creation brings
To light as heralds of His truth
The monarch of the dawning age

When First I Saw the Red-tipped Dawn

When first I saw the red-tipped dawn
Blushing beneath the pale blue sky
I held my breath and waited
For the wonder that I knew would rise

The red blush spread across the ridge
Growing till it filled the air
With crimson clouds tinged deeper purple
Glowing like a living portrait
Brilliantly above the mountaintops
Painted with vivid colors
Shining brighter as the sun
In breath-taking glory
Revealed its stunning rays
Shimmering across the horizon
Turning crimson to orange and gold
With the intensity of its light

I watched the colors melt away
Till only golden light remained
As the sun rose up above the earth
Its golden head too glorious
Too bright to hold my gaze for long

I bowed my head, and looked away
Too weak to bear that wondrous sight
And turned my back to feel the warmth of life
That radiated from its rays
Soaking into my weary frame
Reviving hope inside my heart
That once again I'd seen the dawn

The Silver Dawn

Swirling masses mix with black
Thicker than the foaming seas
Spreading across the darkened sky
Swallowing all in mystery
Devouring what remains of sight
Till nothing lies beneath the gloom
But wisps of white and smokey cloud
Settling down below the rise
To wake up ghostly in the light
Of silver dawn that brightens all
But cannot pierce the veil that hides
And shadows life from searching eyes

The sun, a pale and ghostly form
Attempts to rise, and gain its ground
But the white masses keep it bowed
Diminish its power and tear it down
From its bright and haughty seat of light
Wrapping it up till it hangs forlorn
A phantom of its former glory
A ball of white that barely shines
And barely warms the sleeping earth
That cannot wake from dreamy slumber
Beneath the veil of heavy wonder

The masses keep the sun at bay
But they cannot hold off the day
At noon the swirling clouds disperse
And rise to join the heavens once more
The sun, regaining strength, shines brightly
Piercing the thinning veil with its full might
Recovering lost glory, revealing in its light
Which warms the earth
A blessed sight to weary eyes
Spent long in searching for the sun
To shine its light in the blue skies

Morning Glories

I lay still in quiet slumber
The passing night could not cumber
The sweetness of my dreams, which number
More than I can fathom

Then gentle whispers of the dawn
Shook me, waking me with sweet song
Called me out of darkness, dreaming
Into golden light, which was streaming
Softly, from my window, beaming
Sweetly on my face

I raised my head, my sense regaining
Feeling now the quiet burning
Of delight that set me yearning
For the day ahead

I felt the rush of life returning.
Bounding from my bed, I flew
To gardens beautiful and bright
Filled with fresh new joys of morning
Wonders to my heart's delight!

Cherishing the birdsong's cry
I raised my hands to touch the sky
The joy within my heart complied
To join creation's song anew!

What Bright Skies!

What bright skies in the morning!
As gentle blossoms blow
Amid the wind that carries the song
Of lovers to and fro
Awakening the world
As they zoom across the blue
Merry in their chase
Caught in the rapture of dawn!

The golden light
A joyful sight!
Bleary eyes from sleep receive
A welcome beam of heart's delight
The glory of heaven's might!

The still breath of morning
Washes fear
Cleanses hearts, and makes them hear
The quiet call of nature's song
The gentle whisper of the earth

What echoes dawn
The great love song
That beats the heart of nature's sigh
Creation's hope in every hill
The joy of light in manger still
The promise of the eastern rising
Glory twice before the sun
Everlasting
All is won

A Morning's Symphony

Stretched across the sky,
Painted in layers,
The clouds in formation
Hail bright morning's day!

From liquid gold on the horizon,
The sky erupts into color!
Harmonies of red and orange,
Pink and purple,
Combine their musical notes
Into one great symphony
Of light and joy!

The earth rejoices as the great sun
Raises its glorious mantle,
Spreading its power across the sky,
Awakening the cries and calls
Of all living creatures,
Joined together in sheer wonder
Of the majesty before them.

Together they stand,
Hailing the spectacle,
Delight in their song,
Praise in their throats.

Together they cry,
"Oh glorious morning!"
"Oh majestic dawn!"
"All hail thy Maker,
"The Artist of light!"

Oh Fairest Shines the Morning!

The golden light
On sun-kissed height
Bathes the trees in soft delight
Brighter than honey
Sweeter than sight
Oh fairest shines the morning!

Lady fair
A morning rare
Unequal to jewels of time compare
While the reigning queen
In her rising
Crowns the sky with glory!

Royal blue and brilliant white
The lady fair and queen of light
Rising together, revealing the sight
Of nature's mantle, green and bright!

Oh fairest shines the day!
The sky in lovely array
In flowing robes like the sea
Marvelous in her beauty!

Oh fairest shines the sun!
The queen of day when all is done
In radiance too fair for sight
Fairest beauty at its height!

Oh fairest of fair!
What makes them fair?
The morning blue, the bright-white star
Far fairer than these
The fairest of all
Creation's Maker,
And her heart's call

Oh Celestial Morning!

The sky,
When crisscrossed with streams of gold,
Blends into the fathomless sea of light,
A great delight to the eye of man,
The wonder of the morning sun!

As clouds surround, light shines forth
In streams like blessings
Shining upon the face of the earth,
Veiling the sky in celestial glory,
Calling forth the colors of nature,
The orchestra of heaven's hues!

The sea of gold,
Deep, impenetrable light
Like liquid gold, pours forth,
Bathing all in hope renewed
Like the dying sun's resurrected mantle,
Adorning the sky with grace and beauty!

The dawn,
The sweet, rapturous dawn!
Hailed by all creation, that dawn
Of eternal rising
All nature hails that light of infinite lasting
To outstrip the dawn
And make morning shine forever!

Bright and Glorious Dawn

Oh, dawn!
Oh, bright and glorious dawn!
Like a graceful fawn,
You cross the sky,
Trailing fire,
Light and spry,
Rosy fire or flaming gold
A wondrous sight to behold!

Rising up,
Your flame of glory
Drowns the sorrows of the dark
Hatred's night is put to flight
Love's dawn reigns supreme

The dawn reveals a world of wonders
A marvelous presence now unfolds
The never-ending story flows
From heaven's bright horizon,

The mystery that brings each dawn
A journey deep, but not forlorn
A destiny beyond all hope
A future far secured

The journey that you take today,
Be it far, or just to stay,
Remember that the only way
Lies in one Christ, the Redeemer

How Bright the Sun!

How bright the sun!
As morning dawns,
The red tint of time
Sheds its majesty across the sky,
Spreading its cloak of many colors
To light the clouds,
Their robes aflame!

Finer gold hath no man than the sun!
Its essence is purer than the mines!
Its presence is kingly,
Like a monarch reigning high
How vast is the sun's domain!

That celestial orb
Shining over all,
Whose garb is that of crimson and of fire,
Reflects that glorious Maker,
Whose light makes the sun a shadow,
A pinprick of that awesome glory
That sits in heaven above!

The Sun in Its Courses

The sun in its courses,
Like galloping horses,
Races across the sky,
Arriving triumphantly at day's end,
Erupting into many colors,
Victorious and bright,
Spectacular before the night
Swallows its glory in darkness,
The colorless ink of sleep,
Drowning the noises of daytime in slumber,
Exhausting the memory of sunlight
Till nothing remains but blackness.

The quiet land lies still,
Wakeful as in a dream,
Eager for what it cannot name,
Restless as it searches
Up and down the hilly slopes,
Across the ridges without hope,
Seeking what it cannot see,
Longing for what it cannot remember.

The land lies fitful,
Tossing and turning,
As anxiously it awaits the burning
Of sunlight falling on the earth,
The light of dawn,
That glorious birth!
Of radiant sunshine, swift and true,
To start the race and course anew!

At last, the great heart lifts its head,
That long-awaited glorious red,
Erupting light across the sky!
The sun, its course to live and thrive!

Moonlight Poems

Moonrise

Cool breezes wash through the soft green,
Turning up the leaves, stirring them to dance
As pretty chirps of dusk echo across the field,
Mixed with the quiet rumble of distant sounds,
Barely disturbing the gentle peace of evening.

The blue sky deepens as dark approaches,
Signaling the last light of the sun, and praising
The full-rising moon, silent above the trees,
Watchful as clouds fade to color, then shadow.

The still forms of trees dip their boughs
To the passing breeze,
Revering day's end,
Welcoming night's dawn and mantle
Of calming peace, yet wakeful awe.

As stars climb the heavens, that merry host
Arrayed in brightness
Pierces the dark
With shining hope,
Turning the eye to wonder
At their appearance and form,
Causing breath
To shudder and go out at the majesty
Of their constellation and light.

The beauty of nighttime stalls each passerby,
Making him take in creation's mystery,
Enticing him to hear nature's cry, soft
In the depths of shadow, yet worshipful
As in a hallowed place,
Where small choirs
Gather to offer praise in many tongues.

The deep aura of silent wonder lingers on
As nighttime passes by on quiet feet,
Disturbing nothing waking,
Going till the dawn
Of light calls it to rest,
Awakening new hope
And desire for better things yet to come.

Softly Falls

Softly falls the dark of night
Gently stealing daylight's sight
Clothing all in deepening gray
Turning sunlight into shadow

Quiet slumber steadily creeps
Leaving nothing in its wake
Taking all as midnight's slaves
The quiet merriment delays

Sleepless, I walk through the night
Though slumber beckons all
Wide awake, I take to sight
The beauty and the awe

The brilliant moon
That radiant queen
Whose brightness darkness cannot sway
Shines faithfully upon the bay
Where slumber claims the water's keep

Out on the shore, I see the sky
Still, yet merrier than the day
A host of dazzling courtiers stayed
Arrayed in light to see the queen

Their shimmering robes, alive and bright
Send sparkling rays in dancing flight
Out onto slumber's darkened bay
To pirouette, spin, and play
Each laughing lord and lady white
Sings harmonies, and shines their might
As with their shadows, they do dance
The dance of light, and night's romance.

Before this spectacle, I fall
Lost to speaking and to tongue
My heart beats louder than a gong
And yet my eyes see brighter still
Of all my ears can hear, and fill
Of all my senses, I command
To soak up glory's richest hand

In the Golden Hour

In the golden hour,
When the sun-tipped clouds
Meet to kiss the earth
With radiant colors,
The brown thrasher
Sings his last notes
To a dying day,
Soon to be shrouded in darkened slumber

The pearls of the sky
Reflect the splendor of the tired king
Who shines his glory one last time
Before resting his noble head below the earth
In silence, and in shadow

When the king's light fades, and is gone
The lovely queen of night arrives
With her snowy appearance
Attended by myriads of servants
Sparkling like diamonds
Twinkling brightly
Guarding the night with their precious light
Delighting in the radiance of their queen
As she shines
Bright before the clouds
Or covered in robes of darkness
As the clouds shroud over her
Hiding her light
Amid the sorrow of the stars
As they mourn the loss
Of her lovely light

Then out once more!
The queen of night sings forth her song
As she emerges from her cloudy chambers
Radiant as ever
Delighting her attendants as they surround her
Shimmering brightly in joyful acclamation
Of her lovely presence

She sings till morning light
Calls her to slumber
Her shining robes grow heavy and dull
She sinks her head below the earth
As the glorious king emerges
Adorning the sky with color
Anointing the ground with life and light
Reviving the beasts and plants
As they lift their heads
To give thanks for another day!

Lilac Night

Be still.
The lilac night has fallen.
Dreamy skies
Full of starry eyes
Twinkling,
Sprinkling rays of light
On moonfaced watchers
Watching the beaming smile
Of the moon resting on his cloudy pillow.

The gentle swell of airy song,
The lullaby of breath belongs
To quiet winds that round the ear,
Whispering softly,
"Do not fear."

Across the skies,
The starry hosts take flight!
Across the skies like leaping deer,
Graceful, shooting, soaring clear
Through heaven's veil,
A piercing wonder
Nature's thrilled delight is shown,
The shadows lifted,
Light be known!

Oh marvel of the midnight sky!
Oh wonder of the waking eye!
The beauty of the heavenly hosts
Creation's song of rapture sung
To heaven's hailed, all-glorious King
For whom all hope in nature rings
A song of joyful assonance
A thankful breath of reverence
A voice in one great rolling tide
Crying loudly,
"All praise with Thee abide!"

Bright-Eyed Midnight

In the evening, all is peaceful
The blue calm
Stretches across the endless horizon
Still as breath
Quiet as the dusk
Which creeps up with its rosy fingers
Tinting the sky in blissful color
Of red, orange, purple, and yellow
All blending together
Deepening as the sun goes down
Leaving the earth, which waits
For the cool, refreshing cover of darkness
Which steals across the sky
Silent as shadow
Shrouding all in mystery and expectation

As darkness falls
The sky opens its many eyes
Bright and twinkling
Blinking or streaking with white fire
Above the still form of nature's slumber
Sleeping under the faithful watch
Of night's great guardians

The sky, an ever-present majesty
Stands still above the cold earth
Emanating awe and wonder
From the wakeful eyes of a watching child
Restless in slumber
Dreamless at midnight

Barefoot, he treads across the open fields
Alive with the midnight breeze
Tickling the dandelions
Brushing the grass tips
Whispering to the river
As it flows quietly down the side
Of a lonely hill
Going gently
Mirthless
Still and silent as ink
Passing over rocks and crevices
Hidden beneath the clammy cold
Shrouded in darkness and shadow

The dark water flows
Beneath the spectacle of midnight
Alive with the twinkling presence
Of myriads of stars
All shining, pulsing
Emitting joy and comfort
To the lonely child
Who finds himself at loss for wonder
As he gazes upon the mystery
Of God's creation

Midnight Rides

Silently, the midnight rides
Upon the steady ocean tide
Gently tossed by a whispering breeze
Echoing softly round the trees
That dip their boughs in graceful bends
Beneath the fullness of the moon
That shines upon the quiet shore
Letting its light pour out
Upon the rocks and snowy shells
That lie beneath the sand,
Their edges twinkling like the stars
That sprinkle the sky like lemon drops,
Sweetly patterning the night
With lovely figures made of light.

Their graceful arches, and gentle curves
Dance across the great horizon,
Beaming upon the darkened sea,
Creating patches of merry blues
And sparkling whites,
Mixing together in the gentle stir
Of salty water
That laps and lulls
Beneath the pull of moonlight's call.

The quiet breeze surrounds the shore,
Whispering merrily to creatures
Hiding beneath the rocky outcrops,
Seeking shelter from the nightly hunters
Flying low across the ground,
Their beady eyes searching round
For any sign of movement
Beneath the pearly grains that cover all.

Merry Midnight beams her rays
Upon the beach once fit for play
Observing lost and left behind
Trinkets from occupants long gone.
A single parasol lies half-buried
Beneath the sand at center shore,
Its white lining flapping briefly
In the breeze that tickles round its edges.
A lonely beach ball bounces once
Pushed by impish winds
Which round and round it make a game
To knock it over twice again.

When satisfied with gentle play,
Midnight softly steals away,
And lets the night grow long and dark,
Lingering upon the shore,
Resting in a blissful peace
Until the blushing rays of sun
Push away the dark, and bring
Life and light back to the shore.

Midnight Calm

In the golden hour,
When twilight tints the peaceful sky,
The pretty birds chirp softly and clearly
In the tops of the trees now swaying
In the gentle breeze of lullabies,
Washing over the little flowers of the field,
Cooling their delicate petals
From the ragged heat of the midday sun.

The little blossoms bow their heads
As nightime's slumber blankets them
With peaceful darkness.
It shrouds the ground with shadow,
Covering the earth with cool, sweet rest
As the blissful moonlight soothes
The creatures lulled to sleep by its gentle rays.

The breeze of night, in mercy,
Calms the earth,
Weary of the heat of day,
Ready to rest in the cool relief
Of midnight's refreshing mantel.
It drapes across the sky,
As welcome as rain upon a sea
Of dry and thirsty crops,
Withering under the merciless rays
Of sunlight beating down
With iron will
To draw up every drop of life
And leave behind nothing
But brown and dying leaves.

But midnight's coolness, like the rain
Restores the earth to health again.
It refills nature's empty chalice until
It overflows and spills out
Upon the ground in thanksgiving.

The earth delights in the blessed light
Of the stars that burn, but give no heat,
Of the moon whose light is bearable
For bleary eyes that wake from sleep
To take a peep at night time's charm,
Then return to slumber in content.

Frozen Nightfall

Awake, awake!
The night is falling!
Dusk, with her chilly fingers
Creeps along the horizon
Snuffing out the warmth of day
Frosting over sunlight's gardens
Stealing breath from every tree
Creeping till her fingers find a handhold
And freeze over all that's bare

Trickling ice prevails
Inching over every meadow
Crusting every flower petal
Encasing every tiny dewdrop
Enslaving all in frost and cold

The light of moonrise holds no heat
For icy landscapes it must greet
Relentless frost unchecked by sun
The breath of every creature won
By hardened meeting of the night

The slippery, slinking, silent spite
That holds in bondage nature's night
Upholds its reign triumphantly
Till lo, in morning's dawn emerges
The grateful sun
With strength to purge
All evil from the captive land
Releasing the grasp of cold's demand
Unveiling all beneath the frost as
The happy morning shines again!

Night's Calm

In the quiet calm of night
The nightingale sings its sad note
Of hope and longing
Swallowed up in the mystery of the night
Cool and calming
Like fireflies drifting through the gentle breeze
Far from chilled summer's flower
Closed and cold in darkness
Waiting to bloom in daylight

The quiet calm of night is still
A hushed breath
Waiting patiently for the break of day
Where unmasked glory rises
Tearing across the sky
To awaken light's brilliant anthem
Of song and soaring!

But hush now.
Night has fallen
Night is still

The calm of night increases
Creeping cicadas crawl up the trees
While lulling voices chirp the nightly breeze
Doe-eyed creatures take their rest
As the guardians of night do their best
To shine through the veil of darkness gently

Hush
Be still
Night has fallen
All is still

Song of the Night

The feet of darkness,
Like indigo, stain the sky,
Soaking up with outstretched toes
The light, devouring all till naught remains
But hazy fog and shadow.

Nocturnal sounds
Echo round the horizon,
Filling the hollow air
With noise,
Eerie yet serene.

The hidden orchestra
Brings to life its instruments,
Lifting cries to the night sky,
Drifting harmonies across the dampened ground,
Peaceful and sublime.

The weight of darkness
Hangs heavy with the veil of sleep
As creatures take their rest beneath
The halo moon,
Shining like a beacon o'er the still sea
Of grass,
Bending in the whispering breeze,
Tossed and toyed by gentle laughter,
The underlying song of night.

Hush.

Be still as night sleeps,
Resting calmly,
Peaceful in slumber
Resting as all lie down to dream.

Nature Poems

Spring Flowers

Spring flowers make sunny hours
Hazy days turn into showers
Lazy rain falls down and down
Creating beauty on the ground

When beauty lifts its head from drinking
Shining like a blossom blooming
Radiance bedazzles all
The many-colored drops of dew
Soaked by sun-absorbing leisure
Greener now to all, a pleasure

Little drops of rain and sun
Little petals tossed by wind
Little beauties fair and bright
Little wonders make things right

All around the Waking World

All around the waking world
The rosy sky turns into gold
As birds sing out
So clear and bright
Their morning song of pure delight
As creatures rise up from their beds
To marvel at the rising sun

From resting slumber
All will come
To see the rising of the sun
That star of light that gives out life
And burns with hope in the dawning day
With blessings pouring from each ray
To warm and comfort all the earth

That sun
With laughing joy does come
And lends a hand in giving birth
To seedlings young and strong to grow
And spread their blooms out to the sky
Echoing the joyous cry
Of springtime conquering the earth!

As springtime comes and fades away
The sun remains, and longs to stay
Through lazy summer's dragging hours
Picking up the fresh-laid flowers
And scattering their seeds through wind
As hot and humid settles in
The hazy green and grassy days
Of summer peace and simple ways

As summer stretches into fall,
The humid fades,
And green withdraws
The wind picks up a pinch of cold,
And autumn's leaves turn into gold.
The autumn fades.
The leaves all fall,
With nothing left but dirt and barren ground.
The sun retreats,
And naught remains
But empty trees
And biting chill.

Then, as the frost is settled in
The sun emerges yet again
The winter changes into rain
And springtime claims the earth again

Softly I Steal Away

Softly I steal away
To better fields of green
Where daffodils play instruments,
A strange and lively tune
Upon their petals sprayed with dew,
The mystic morning dust of spring.

I watch the fairies flitting through
The colored masses, sweet and true,
Anointing them with fairy dust,
Creating life and bloom.

Still I lie as clouds go by,
Fluffy pink and yellow
Across the brilliant sky of blue,
Lighter than feathers, freer too.

The mystic world behind my eyes,
The visions that I devise,
Brighten my days with longings fair,
Creating light and beauty rare.

The visions deep within my mind,
Imagination's ringing chime,
Beckon each moment a newer thought,
Still and silent, yet begotten,
With mystery and deep romance
As though my heart lay in a trance,
Entwined in longing's lingering bower,
Unable to rest till words flow free,
Mixing their magical harmony
With vision's enticing melody.

Light with Glory Shines

Lazy morning clouds drift over the blue haze
Of breathy sky as sunlight lifts its fingers
And points to those floating fields of snow,
Turning them to gold in its warmth and glow.

The golden landscape, mixed with crimson,
Shines upon the waking world
As slumber sheds its blanket,
And dawn calls with the larking of the day.
Strange and brilliant cries fill the air with life,
Coloring the wind as the sun clothes the sky,
Bright and shrill in their harkening
To draw out weary creatures with the allure
Of their early woven songs.

Shimmering light plays upon blue
Dancing across the waves,
Merry in its chase of wonder,
Inviting the eyes to look and behold
Its pretty array, fairylike and pure.

Swirling mists adorn the rising green
Like delicate robes, wispy and elegant,
Crowning the mountains with halos of white,
Majestic and serene.

The morning light with glory shines,
Echoing a bliss sublime,
Revealing beauty, creation's awe,
A priceless jewel, a gift for all
Who see the awesome power of dawn
And wonder at the Creator's song.

Fog

Heaven's blanket weighs down
The earth beneath,
Its thick white folds engulfing Earth's surface,
Till all is wet in its embrace.

Milky mist,
Rising from the ground,
Meets the sky, and turns to whiteness.
All is shrouded;
Barely a whisper of life remains unaltered
By the heavy presence of all-consuming fog.

Barely a foot is seen.
All paths are taken step by step.
Each step reveals new sight,
But one step at a time.

As fog on Earth, so fog within.
The path you take, take step by step.
Mistakes are made when rushed ahead.
Remember and be patient.

A Drowsy World

Gloomy clouds hung above a graying lot,
Drizzling a constant rain, wet and dreary,
Upon a drowsy world
Ready to fall back into slumber
At the slightest lull of the gray wind
That drifted lazily across the dull stone.

A starling in lonely flight
Arched its way across the sky,
Its cry unheard in the weary masses
That barely concealed its slender form.

The Conquering Blow

In the blue calm,
A little cloud hovers above the horizon
Unnoticed by the world below,
Mysterious in its lonely presence
Upon the mountain ridge.

It waits patiently,
While the high and mighty sun
Pours forth its boastful rays
Upon the gladened land,
Promising fullness of wealth
In its shining glory.

It quietly remains,
Undaunted
By the taunts of sunlight.
Little by little,
It gathers strength
From the four winds,
Growing till it becomes
A dark and foreboding mass,
Blotting out the arrogant sun,
Threatening to fall upon the earth
Without mercy.

Without the sun's protection,
The earth waits
As the first drops of ice
Fall upon the barren ground,
Shattering into a thousands slivers,
Sharp and jagged as they pierce the dirt.

The sky rumbles in anticipation
As its shores turn black as the sea,
Stricken by the occasional flash
Of lightning as it snakes down,
Striking the ground,
And sending out jolts of energy
Strong enough to fry the trees that sway
Helplessly in the winds that rise,
Moaning as the momentum of their pattern
Increases by titanic magnitude.

The storm roars with ferocious power,
Tearing down everything in its path,
Flinging the dead weight of trees
Miles above the ridge,
Sucking up debris into the funnel
Of awesome strength
That towers above the mountain,
Devastating the terrain like a chaotic plague
That preys upon its victims,
Villainous and cruel.

The monstrous gale shrieks
Like a triumphant beast
As it finishes its rampage
Over the mountain range,
Wildly delighting in its success
At destroying what once was whole.

Satisfied with his raid,
The conqueror rides to other conquests,
Leaving behind a pillaged land,
Bruised and bleeding from the thrashing
Of the winds that tore, and broke it to pieces.

The suppressed sun returns,
And seeks to aid in the restoration
Of the weak and wounded mountain,
Whose battle scars will never fully heal,
And will carry the memories
Of the fatal blows that beset and subdued
The aching ridge
With their raw and jealous might.

Misted Storm Tide

From the misted harbors,
Awakens slumber!
See the rising of the stars!
Feel the dancing of the wind!
Witness the moving of mountains,
The rush and wail of the sea,
As it crashes over valleys,
Rolls over hillsides,
Runs over drylands,
Till all is consumed in its chaotic energy!

The whirlpool and the storm bow
Before the hurricane of madness,
Dipping and churning reality
Till its monstrous head blows
Under the vast canvas of purple-bruised night,
Yawning to receive the victories of chaos,
Sucking up time's emotions
Till the sea of nightmares turns to solitude
And insanity dwindles to calm and quiet.

Then still the waters under the sudden flood
Of starlight!
Piercing down upon the wreckage left by fear,
Consuming all darkness, till night is dancing
With the brilliance of joy!
Radiating hope upon forsaken,
Beaming peace upon worn cares.

The night, in its stillness and beauty,
Reigns calmly over the sea.
No more the havoc of storms
Churns the waters till they're bloated,
Unsettling the serenity of lady midnight,
Whose steady hand holds sway
Over gentle tide
As it breathes in and out,
Softly, and in slumber.

The peace of midnight is sealed.
All is quiet.
Rest.

The Beauty of the Rain-Washed Earth

The beauty of the rain-washed earth
That dewy sea of green
That catches rays of heaven's light
Adding to its sheen
The sparkling drops of heaven's love
Adorning every blade
Shimmering like crystal cups
All shattered, yet displayed

The dewy blossoms of the morning
Radiate the dawning sky
And catch the pulse of heaven's beating
Dazzling like a diamond eye

Awake, oh wonder
See the sky!
Reflect, oh mortal eye, on high!
The simple jewels of water shine
Yet treasures purer than these find
In simple nature, still, reborn

Awake, oh mortal
See your life!
Of beauty and of truth, take sight!
Let hope within you be your light
Awake, dear heart
Embrace your life!

A Woven Wildness

In a tangle of branches
Spry and slim
I clung to every limb
Easing my way upwards
Into the canopy of madness
That surrounded me with interlocking arms
And many fingers that pointed
In every direction
Creating a woven harmony that enthralled
My wild spirit
And drew me up
Into the sky
Sharp and clear
As it shone down through the leaves
Piercingly blue
Brilliant with the sun that sat
Behind a cloud
White and glorious
Calling my heart to sing
With the cries of the creatures
That rang out in all tongues
Mixed with the wind that rose and fell
Stirring the song with its whispering
Rousing a dance with its passing
Thrilling my mind with its whirring
Gently, softly round my ears

Ride on the Wings of Dawn!

Ride, ride, ride on the wings of dawn!
The freeing wind to you is drawn.
Spirit wild, reckless, free
Without restraint of enmity.

Ride, ride, ride on the wings of the wind!
Breathless, free, alive as can be!
Fearless as fire and light
Shunning all of dark and night.

Ride, ride, ride on the wings of the sun!
Its flame a guide to spur you on.
Its light an assurance fierce and true.
The hope of rising ever new.

Ride, ride, ride on the wings of truth!
Seek all that is sight
Flee far from the night
Take hold of the light!

Thoughtful Poems

Within the Silver Lining

Within the silver lining of reality
Come forth, my poetic phrase!
"Come out, and make a river!"
"Come forth, and pour out a song!"

Once upon a memory
Twice upon a dream
There was a little stream that flowed
That turned into a river
That turned into an ocean
Of words whose power shook
And rocked the boats
Of fishermen, now forced to swim
Through currents
That surrounded them
With watery melodies
Bubbling and churning merrily

Then darkness came
And tempests blew
The bubbling ocean grew and grew
Till it brewed a hurricane
No longer merry, but fierce,
Violent, and cruel!

The song of the ocean turned
To pounding and ear-splitting tunes
That wreaked havoc on its listeners
And punished its occupants
With chaotic dance
As waves tossed to and fro
Delirious in chaotic pleasure
Intent on destructive measure

With every rise and fall
Their dance became wilder still
The waves leapt and crashed
Alive with panic
Desperate with passion!

The fishermen cried
As the water spun its torturous song
Of chaos
Frenzied and furious
Foaming with raw power
As it sought to overtake all in its path

And then...
As though in a trance,
I awoke, and saw no more
Only peace, the quiet calm of dawn
The breaking of day by ocean breeze
The silent call of nature
As it unfurled its light
From under the heavy blanket of darkness

The world stood before me
Shining and bright
No longer tempest
No longer night

The peace of the hour upon me still
I shall awake, and see no more ill

Poetry is Woven Insight

A poem is a group of sentences
Woven together by colorful words
Splashing the page with bright meaning
Or moving mystery
Enticing the reader to dig in
For further insight
Into the threads of time and space
Spun intricately into a pattern of beauty
That cuts into the edges of reality
Or folds into the mind of thoughts
Churning and burning with the flames
Of passion spun
For such moments
As when passion's fancies encroach
Upon the mind at rest
Turning it on to produce structured thought
That builds a maze of locks and doors
Opening and closing at odd angles
Never quite straight
But always
Leading to another place
Where feet may run, and turn again
Back through the door to the outside realm
Where thought and structure align
With the course of reason rather than fancy

Lonely in the Woods of Pondering

Lonely in the woods of pondering,
I wandered like a deer disturbed,
Seeking refuge in the caves
Of buried hopes and hidden dreams.

I stumbled weary like a doe
Who's been about in heavy snow,
Nosing round for autumn's leavings,
Finding naught but apple cores
Frozen hard by nature's frost,
Bitten brown by bitter cold.

I dragged my weary frame across
A rocky shelter free from frost.
I fell upon my knees gasping,
Wheezing out my frozen breath.
I found an outcrop, and sat heaving,
Trying to regain my strength,
Which seemed impossible,
So weary was my heart
That I could not fight the sleep
That wrapped around me like a fog,
Drowning out the cold and frostbite,
Dragging me down to hidden shores,
Full of unknown secrets and whispered thoughts.

I dreamt of many things embedded
In the deepest of my thoughts,
Things of hope and worth and measure,
Things of forgotten mystery,
Sparks of light and fantasy
That flitted through my sleeping mind,
Some of which still lingered
When,
I drew my eyes from slumber,
And,
I found myself upon the ledge,
Once more inspired by lost hope.

Lost Things Found

Over hills and under vales
Through stone and mountain
Searching, searching, searching
Under seas and through the sky
Yearning, yearning, yearning
Rocky paths or smooth green grass
Hilly shales or hilltop flowers
Sunny days or morning showers
Open fields or covered bowers
Always searching, always seeking
Yearning, yearning, yearning
In darkest night
Where sheds no light
In vivid day
Where every ray
Illuminates the spectacle
In gloom, in shade
In dark, in space
In light, in day
Seeking
Searching
Longing
Lost things, found things
Which are they?
How to tell?
Where to seek?

When lost things are found
The joy of morning
Blossoms into a musical anthem
That rises to the clouds
Glorious in gladess
Radiant in happiness

Lost is found
Now all is restored
No more searching
All is found
Life is found

The Quiet Joy of Living

The quiet joy of living
Is found in simple pleasure
Deeper than fine treasure
Beyond price or earthly measure

The peace of daily living
The steadiness of time
The simple joy of giving
Echoes the sublime

The gentle warmth of caring
A song of love begotten
The gentle heart loves sharing
Each piece of truth divine

Still

The sun rises gently
Breaking the night with blushing light
Revealing a world of wonders
Precious gems uncovered from their darkness
Sparkling with morning dew
Dripping with newness of life
Still in their waking
Still as if waiting
Still

As a breeze wafts to and fro
Lifting the graceful boughs of trees
Still

As waves dip toward the shore
And then recess
Still

As the many wings of butterflies
Drift up high into the skies
Still

As a single grain of sand falls
Splashing into the same-colored sea
Blending till undistinguished
Completely absorbed in the fold
Still

All around is still
Still without
And still within

Still in waiting
Still in hoping
Still in believing
Still in trusting
Still

A Little Sprout

I looked upon a world of night,
Gripped by fear, the devil's fright,
Muddied in misery,
Shrouded in sorrow,
Buried in sight of no tomorrow

I looked, and saw all hope was dead
Nothing remained but tombstone heads,
Solid and gray, broken and burned,
No source of light to ease their pain
Amid the black and broken stone,
I saw a seed lying forlorn
Upon a ground of sooty ash,
Limp and lifeless, abandoned trash

I picked it up, and felt a thrum
A gentle tingling, slightly warm
It was as though a life destroyed
Were resurrecting from the grave

I dug a hole, and laid it down,
Covering it with sooty ground
And left it lying in the dust,
Leaving it to break and die

The sunlight fell upon its form,
And so did fall the gentle rain
And day by day, it yearned to rise
To greatness and kiss the light of the sun

At last, its little figure came,
Dropped upon by gentle rain
One tiny leaf had all to gain,
The little sproutling drank the rain

Day by day, the sproutling grew
Taller, stronger, and greater too
Till once a sprout now stood a sapling
Shaking its many leaves about,
Bending its trunk when tempests sprung,
But never too weak to break or shatter

The sapling grew into a tree
Lodging its roots securely
In deeper ground past soot and ash,
A firm foundation found at last,
Steady, still, unmoving, fast

Whispered in Light

In Winterland, a quiet voice
Echoes through the misty lights,
Whispering, beckoning,
Telling of wonders behind the veil
Of clouded reality

It calls,
Drawing all with ears
And open hearts
To step into the wintry madness
And become lost in the chaos of lights,
Twinkling,
Sparkling,
Glittering,
Gleaming with treasures hidden from sight
Of all but the eyes of dreamers.

A dream may be stronger
Than the shadows of day
Its steps are more sure
Than those waking who stay
Grounded in darkness,
Unwilling to walk
In the mystery of light, bright and compelling

Getting lost is the miracle of wonder.
To be dazzled by beauty,
Cut from raw power,
Shattering feeble vision
Till all is lost in brightness
And in awe,
Is to be lost in light!
It is better than groping in blackness.

Being swallowed by wonder
Is fiercer than the gnawing of shadow.

The light lies open for all to receive,
For all to embrace its beauty and luster!

For light beckons all
Its presence is strong
Its brightness takes all
Till all is lost in its glory.

Why Does the Light Shine Brighter?

Why does the light shine brighter
In places dark and deep
Where fear builds castles fierce and strong
With misery in their keep?

Why does the light shine stronger
In voids evading sight,
Where sorrow cries in silent pain
And shields the aching heart?

Why does the light shine fuller
In depths of burnt despair,
Where hope is gone, naught to be found
But wood and rotting nails?

A cross of grief lies broken,
But broken cannot break
The promised light that was to live
And make our suffering quake

The tomb lies empty, buried
Beneath a long-lost hope
A resurrection twice to tell
The end of night's condemning hell
The rise of morning's hopeful dawn
The peace of living life in bloom

The Winding Path

The winding path leads up a hill
To places sweet and gentle still
To meadows soft, and hollows bare
Devoid of every grief and care.

Yet through the woods this road must pass
Through twists and trunks of broken glass
Through places lost to sun and hope
Left only dark and without sight
Without a word, without a sound
A hopeless woe-beguiled ground.

Though shadows fall, and visions blur,
Destination's hope endures
The fruitful peace of heaven's green
The joy of everlasting brings
A quiet confidence secured,
A trust to rest, and faith assured

Little Cares

When little cares begin to grow,
And stretch their claws out till they pierce,
Creating agony and tears,
Relentless in their biting, fierce,
We cry out to the Lord above,
Beseeching aid, consuming love
To drown the throbbing and the pain
Desiring mercy's blessed rain
To heal the sting of nature's mark
And help us as we now embark
Once more on heaven's trail of bread,
Ever seeking to be fed
By gentle hand and gracious rod,
The Shepherd leading us abroad
Or in our homestead soft and still,
The nature of our Maker's will
To bring all souls to Zion's bliss,
Salvation's off'ring with a kiss
Of holy pardon, sweet and sure,
The hope of all eternal, pure
The promise that for all is told,
A heritage and crown of gold

All Remains but Lost a Moment

To wait is hard, and often long
It sings a dull, and boring song
Or sometimes a soft and gentle beat
Keeping time with steady feet
The rhythm of the path of plenty
Sloping upward bit by bit
Till time in due receives its price
And patience comes to peace at last.

But lo, the path lies thick and thorny
Suffering cannot abide
The pinch and pricking of its hide
The fitful steps of sorrow bleary
Meeting travelers weak and weary
Tearing down the strongest hearts
Panicking the steady soul
Groaning deep as hurt remains
Anxious, eager for hope's gain.

Hope, though slow and long in coming,
Will at last be met by running,
Leaping, joyful hearts of mirth
Lavishing on heaven's turf
Rejoicing in the heat of the sun
Which never sets and never burns
Undying days of gladness coming
Living joy and peace forever.
To wait is waiting but a moment
All will pass, and yet remain
The truth of hope and heaven's gain
Is simple faith in He who reigns.

Fears Fall Down

When fears fall down, and break the ground
They grow deep roots to shake the sound
To break each faith, and take each goal
And make it seem an empty hole
A barren ground of fruitless hopes
A wasteland of dejected gain
A grainless field, no seed to sow
A rotten landscape of woe
A tree with branches thin and snapped
A sapless hollow of regret

But faith takes root not in the shaking
In nothing less than whole, nonbreaking
Peace of God, the quiet pool
The gentle stream of running grace
The broader rivers of hope's race
The deeper oceans of God's love
Surrounding, crowning all above
With radiant beauty that endures
That seeks to finish all that cures
That walks the steady ground assured
And lets all fear take flight unheard

We Do Not Walk in Tears of Fear

We do not walk
In tears of fear,
That crying worry
With its biting edge,
Stealing our peace and consolation,
Turning our contemplation
From surer paths,
The straight and narrow,
To twisted trails
Of dust and rubble,
Full of ruts and hidden hollows,
Yawning in wait for those who stumble,
Caught in their unsteady treading,
Trapped in the snare,
Crushed by each care,
That hopelessness of ceaseless winding
That echoes loud at every bend
We do not walk
In fruitless doubting,
Whose limbs bear nothing
If not rotting
Wantonness, which leaves us longing
Emptiness, which leaves us grappling
With each want and empty hand
But we will walk
On steady hope
Fixed ahead, no need to grope
The path lies clear and confident
Serene, each grace we find in store
And mercies keeping evermore

Love Is Not Grudging

Love is not grudging.
It holds not a thing.
Yet its chalice is pleasant and full.
It flows from bright waters
Into long, flowing streams
Into bottomless oceans.
And still, love goes on.

It caves not to aggression,
Loss, or depression.
For love is made stronger through woe.
It holds not to hostility,
But gives out hospitably.
For love is the hostess of care.

It never falters.
Is steady at the altar.
For love is living in prayer.

It does not stop believing,
Hoping, and cleaving
To heaven's bright promise,
Redemption's great flame.

It holds to the end,
Unbending,
Unchanging
For love is stronger
And fiercer than death.

Stand in Humble Triumph

Shield your heart with faith and sword
The devil and his demons ward
With prayer and grace abiding hence
In Jesus' gift of sustenance
His holy mantle, red and pure
Salvation's garment ever sure
The robes of kingly justice granted
To a heathen, rich or poor

Walk with God

Walk with God
Don't be afraid
Let go of doubt, and turn to trust
Let go of homespun worry's thread
And feast on heaven's daily bread

The best of choice, the sweetest frame
Partaking in that blessed name
Of Jesus dear, yet little sought
Of God the Father was begotten
Was born of virgin mother kind
Was laid in lowly manger minded
By the cattle and the sheep
Met by shepherds there to see
The promise of the star above

The wise men followed with their love
Brought many gifts, and laid them bare
At the feet of the manger with care
Declared the glory of His birth
Proclaimed His sovereignty and worth
The blessed King to reign o'er all
To give His life for ransomed fall
To restore to health what once was sick
To reap a harvest in the thick
Of sin and sorrow
Suffering, want
A fruitful bounty
Blessed and bound
By fair redemption's gracious crown
A promise and a blessed keep

Our Savior, Lord, His children meets
With loving care and tender zeal
His occupation true and real
Fatherlike, He tends and spares
For He is Lord,
The God who cares

What Good We Own

What good we own
If not of Christ
Is filth and rags
Cannot suffice
To pay the price of blood once shed
Upon a cross stained deep with red

Of what we boast
If not of God
Is wasted gain
Not worthy of
It is not praise, nor adoration
It is but man's vain habitation

What hope we seek
If not the Lord
Is hopeless thought
Pierced by a sword
It is the cry of desperation
To a void without salvation

What life we live
If not of Christ
Is emptiness
A rocky bed
A stream devoid of living water
An existence without a founder

Be Still in Eventide

Be still in eventide
When darkness shakes the veil of night
Covering all hope and light
With nothingness, the empty void
Yet hope remains, is not destroyed

The quiet flicker of the flame
The burning whisper of a name
That turns the ashes into sparks
That rise until they become part
Of a greater flame
The rising song
The anthem of all hearts to God!

Across the hills
Across the seas
The peoples cry their desperate pleas:
"Come now!
"Come now
"Hosanna loud!
"Our gracious Lord, who blessed and saved
"Each one of us with voices raised
"In joyful harmony to Him
"Who freed us from the bounds of sin
"Whose hope we offer freely now
"That every sinner's knee may bow
"Before the Lamb, before the throne,
"Eternal life to be made known!"

Come, Misted Havens

From the misted havens, come!
From the shadowed valleys, come!
Come see the thistle and the thorn
The pierced one who, for our sake
    Was born a crying babe
That we might heaven's majesty taste
    And partake in joyous feasting.

From heaven's paradise, He came
    To nest in Earth's dark bower
No regal welcome to proclaim
    He came with no power

A helpless child meek and bare
He came to our weary souls to care
A troubled world, its burdens shared
    He came to save us all

So come, ye weak and heavy-laden
    Come, ye aching hearts, and see
Heaven's peace in a manger lying
    Holiness in a quiet babe

Come see the swaddled king lying
    Tiny infant resting warm
Come, behold the feeble youngling
Heaven's Lord in humble dwelling

Come see the One who greatly loved us
Come, behold the perfect Lamb
Bound for sacrifice, is waiting
Waiting for the great I Am

Come worship Earth's renowned redemption
Come, praise the humble king
Come, receive the blessed telling
Promise, now fulfilled, has come

They Came

Frostbitten and cloth-wrapped,
They came
Weary-footed and travel-sore,
They came
Seeking refuge from the cold, dark world
Seeking hope in the warmth of a manger stall
Seeking life in the light of a child
Seeking joy in the presence of new birth
Seeking comfort in the shadow of the King

They came without cause
No gift, no banner
They came as the poor
The helpless, the bare
They came as the broken,
Distraught, and feeble
To drink deeply of living water
Of heaven's promise fulfilled

They came without nation
The outcasts, the lowly
They came seeking lordship
The King of all kings
They came as the needy
The clinging, the crying
To receive help of helps
From the Healer of all

They came as unworthy
Undeserving of friendship
They came as raw sinners
Their confession laid bare
They came for salvation
The true gift of sacrifice
They came for reception
As children of God

We come as unworthy
All blemished sinners
We come as the stained
The needy of prayer
We come for salvation
The true gift of sacrifice
We come to be children
The redeemed of the cross

Seek the Brighter and the Best

Seek the fruit that grows from the vine
Not the berries that hide among thorns
That pierce when hands are reaching out
Scratching and tearing what once was whole
Leaving a mark, a scar to remember
What once seemed bright, but now is null

Seek the light that shines upon the hill
Not the lantern of the valley's tent
Which seems so warm and beckoning
Till fateful feet reach rock and shale
And stumble into sorrow's veil

The better is the best of sight
Unclouded by the taint of stain
Revealed in heaven's deepest rest
Sought after by the hopeful poor

To seek what will and love what may
Is better than to rise and play
A folly's game of pick and posy
A merry ring-around-the-rosy
That leads away from straight and steady
To rocky paths of painted treasure
Seemingly rich and full of measure
Till the end, which comes too soon
Brings bitter tidings of death and gloom

Life Is a Gift

Life is a gift
The gift that keeps giving
But life at its source
Is eternity's keeping

Life is a joy
The joy beyond wonder
But wonder is still
When infinite reaching

Life is a hope
A hope beyond measure
But hope comes alive
With everlasting pleasure

The gift that we seek
Be we, humble and meek
In joy shall we keep
When the harvest we reap

For All the Blessings

For all the blessings I have seen
For every rock and sunny road
For all the visions I've beheld
I give Thee thanks, oh Lord above
For every shower of Thy love

Each day a gift
Each hour a treasure
To hold, to hope, and take in pleasure
For every gold, there is a measure
For every measure, I give Thee thanks

Much have I seen
Much have I sung
Till I reach long eternity's note
Of blissful blessing evermore
The glory of eternal shore
The never-setting sun of joy

About the Author

Margaret Wade is new to writing, but her passion is inspired by the many books and fantasies she had read while growing up. She graduated from Covenant College with a degree in Spanish, inspired by her love of language and the arts. She has always been fascinated with language and its power to heal and revive. She sees the beauty of words as a portal into the imagination and wonder that lie beneath the surface of all things. Words empower her to speak the truth she knows and holds to as a believer and follower of Christ.

Writing helps her express what she feels she cannot put into normal speech. Through writing, she seeks to empower and encourage others in their walk with Christ, reminding them of the beauty of creation and the mysterious power that dwells within. Her poetry expresses both the natural and the supernatural elements of life and the need for awareness of that which lies beneath the surface.

Margaret is a proud supporter of the arts and hopes to accomplish more in her life both in writing and in music, which she delights in more than just on Sunday mornings. Her musical talent, which she has developed since childhood, has been inspired by her great love of theatrics and her growing aspirations to someday be in a musical. She hopes to make the most of the gifts that God has given her and thanks the support of her friends and family for making her dreams come alive.

Printed in the USA
CPSIA information can be obtained
at www.ICGtesting.com
LVHW090613130524
779900LV00002B/397